Tiny Dinosaurs

By Steven Lindblom
Illustrated by Gino D'Achille

Paul C. Sereno, Consultant
Assistant Professor, University of Chicago

A GOLDEN BOOK · NEW YORK

Western Publishing Company, Inc., Racine, Wisconsin 53404

Millions of years ago huge dinosaurs walked the earth. They were the biggest animals that ever lived on land.

Ultrasaurus (ul-tra-SAWR-us) may have been bigger than a five-story building.

Fierce Tyrannosaurus (tye-ran-o-SAWR-us) was as tall as a telephone pole and weighed as much as a schoolbus. When he ran, the ground must have trembled.

Hiding in the bushes as these monsters thundered by were other, smaller creatures. What were these creatures? Some were lizards, others were small mammals, and others were...

TINY DINOSAURS!
    Not all dinosaurs were giants. Dinosaurs came in
all sizes, just as animals do today. Many dinosaurs
were no bigger than you. Some were even smaller.

Dinosaurs once lived all over the world. Some may have lived right where you live today. But the world did not look like it does now. There were no people, houses, or roads then. Many kinds of strange plants grew everywhere. The weather may have been much warmer than it is now.

Saltopus (sal-TOE-pus) was one of the earliest
and tiniest dinosaurs. It lived 160 million years ago.
Saltopus was only the size of a cat and ate bugs and
lizards. With its long legs it looked like a featherless
roadrunner and must have been very fast.

People used to think of dinosaurs as being great big lizards, but we now know that they were not. Lizards are cold-blooded, and today scientists think some dinosaurs may have been warm-blooded. Many dinosaurs walked on their hind legs, like birds. They carried their tails in the air for balance instead of dragging them on the ground. Lizards cannot do those things.

Compsognathus (comp-so-NATH-us) was a very small dinosaur. It had a close cousin, Archaeopteryx (ar-kee-OP-ter-ix). Both had long tails and sharp teeth. Looking at the bones of these two cousins it is very hard to tell them apart.

But Archaeopteryx also had wings and feathers.
It was a good flier. It may also have been able to
climb trees, using the claws on its wings and legs.

These tiny dinosaurs fed on insects, lizards, and other tiny animals. They were fast and agile. They had to keep out of the way of their hungry bigger cousins.

Being such little animals in a world of giants must have made most of the tiny dinosaurs very timid. They probably lived like mice or chipmunks do today, darting about quietly in search of food.

Not Deinonychus (dine-o-NYE-kus), though. A little smaller than a man, it was one of the fiercest dinosaurs of all. Deinonychus had a mouth full of sharp teeth, and a sharp middle claw on each back foot for slashing. It was very fast and could outrun anything it couldn't eat.

But not all the tiny dinosaurs were meat-eaters. Some ate only plants. Psittacosaurus (sit-a-ko-SAWR-us), or "parrot-lizard," had a powerful beak like a parrot's. It used its beak to eat tough plants and small trees, which it ground up in its stomach with stones it swallowed.

Another plant-eater, Ammosaurus
(am-mo-SAWR-us), was only the size of a large dog.
Like its big cousin Brontosaurus (bront-o-SAWR-us),
it spent most of its time on four legs, although it
could stand and walk on two.

Heterodontosaurus (het-er-o-don-to-SAWR-us) was only the size of a turkey and fed on plants. With its grinding teeth it could eat almost anything. With its biting teeth it could fight off other dinosaurs.

Another tiny dinosaur, Scutellosaurus
(scut-tle-o-SAWR-us), didn't need sharp teeth to
protect itself. Its back was covered with bony armor
plates. Scutellosaurus had a tail that was twice as
long as its body.

Some tiny dinosaurs were tiny because they were babies. Even the biggest of the dinosaurs were tiny when they hatched from eggs. Many dinosaur babies were so small, they would have fit in your hand. Even a newly hatched Brontosaurus was probably smaller than a cat.

You might not recognize a baby Stegosaurus
(steg-o-SAWR-us) unless you saw it with a grown-up
one. Stegosauruses may not have grown their back
plates until they got older.

Maiasaura (mye-a-SAWR-a) was only the size of a robin when it hatched from its egg, but it grew up to be 30 feet long.

How did such big dinosaur mothers ever care for such tiny babies? They must have been very gentle for their size. Scientists used to think that dinosaurs just laid their eggs and left them, the way turtles do today. Now we believe that many dinosaurs fed and cared for their young, the way birds do.

A dinosaur mother was too big to sit on her eggs without breaking them. Instead she covered them with leaves and moss to keep them warm until they hatched.

The little dinosaurs would stay close to the nest
until they were big enough to go off on their own.

Many dinosaurs lived in herds with other dinosaurs like themselves. There would have been many little dinosaurs in the group at one time. Did they play with each other? Maybe they did, chasing each other and splashing about in the water.

The last dinosaurs died out 65 million years ago. You can never see live dinosaurs—just their bones. But many scientists think today's birds are direct relatives of the dinosaurs. So the next time you feed the birds, you can imagine you are feeding tiny dinosaurs!